OCEAN LIFE SPECIAL

Let's DOT ABC with SEA ANIMALS

A Dot and Learn Alphabet Activity book for kids

ages 4-8 years old

little brain

Kindly Subscribe to our newsletter
for future freebies, printables, book launches
and blog articles.
Kindly Make Sure you open our mails
or visit our website frequently. Don't miss out.

visit: www.littlebrainpublishing.com

TermS of Use:

Please do not Share, reproduce or Sell
this freebies to anyone . We reSpect your
honeSty. Any act of piracy will be dealt legally.

THIS BOOK BELONGS TO

Claim Your
Christmas Bonus

Thank you for purchasing our book. To expand your kid's creativity and art skills here is a Holiday Surprise for the little one.

Get a 50 PAGE Christmas Coloring Book for FREE

To Claim Your FREE Coloring Book, kindly visit :

www.littlebrainpublishing.com/bonus

or, email us at
hello@littlebrainpublishing.com
with the picture of this book.

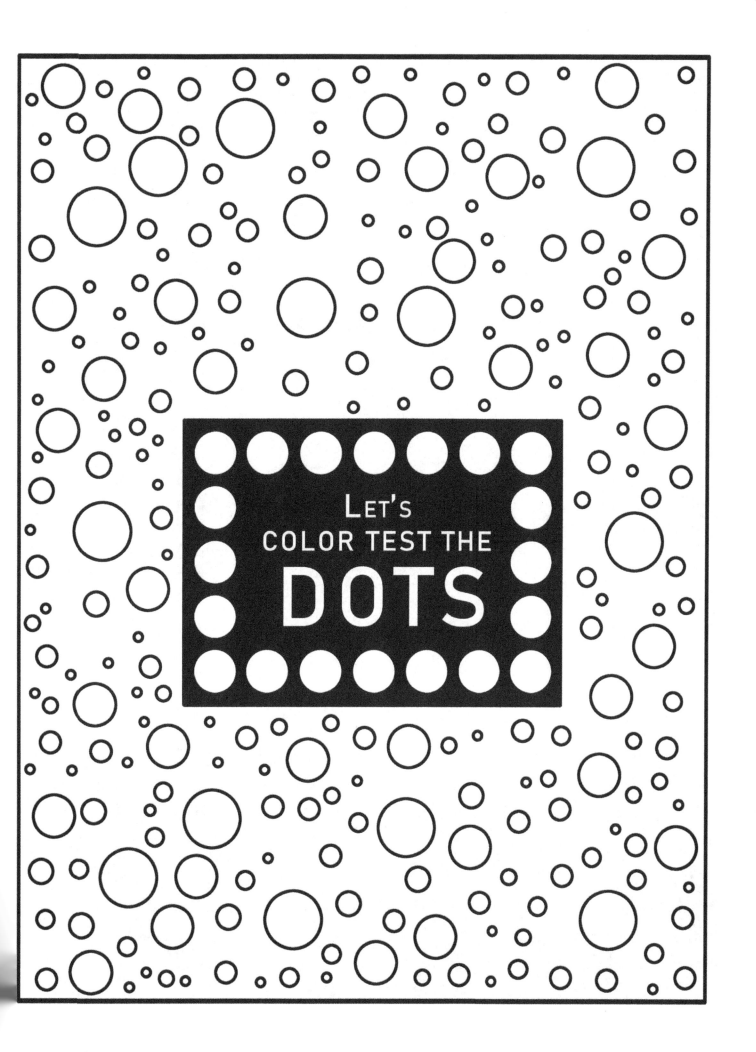

ANGELFISH

BLUE WHALE

CLOWNFISH

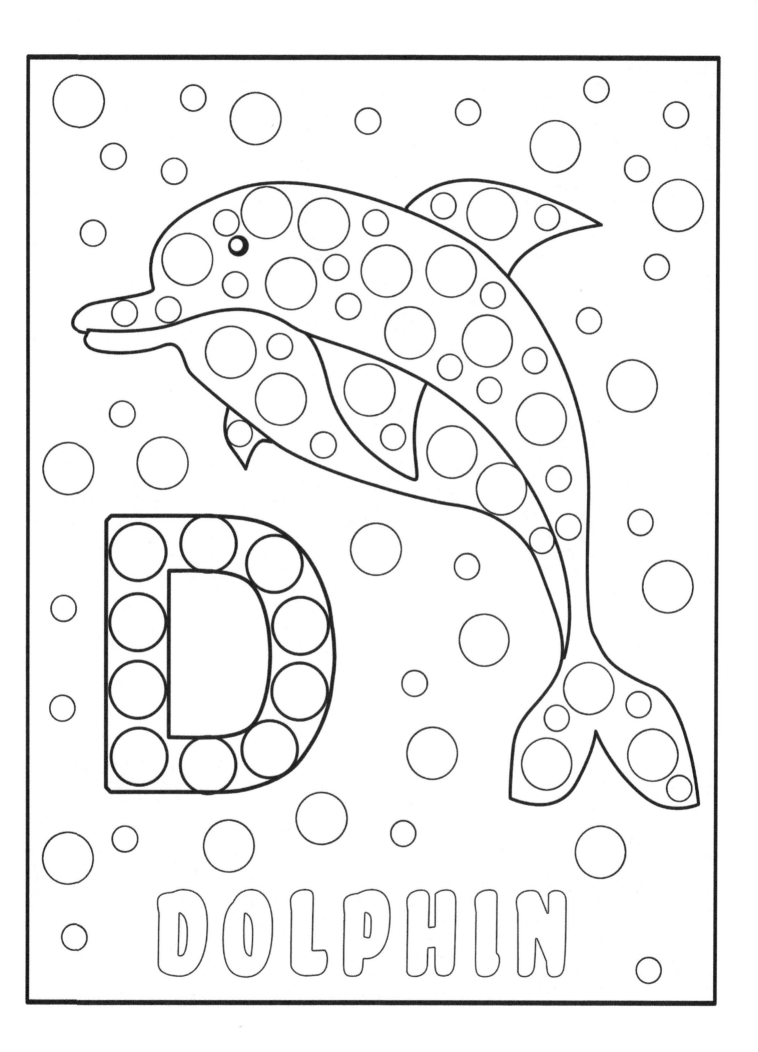

DOLPHIN

GULL

HERMIT CRAB

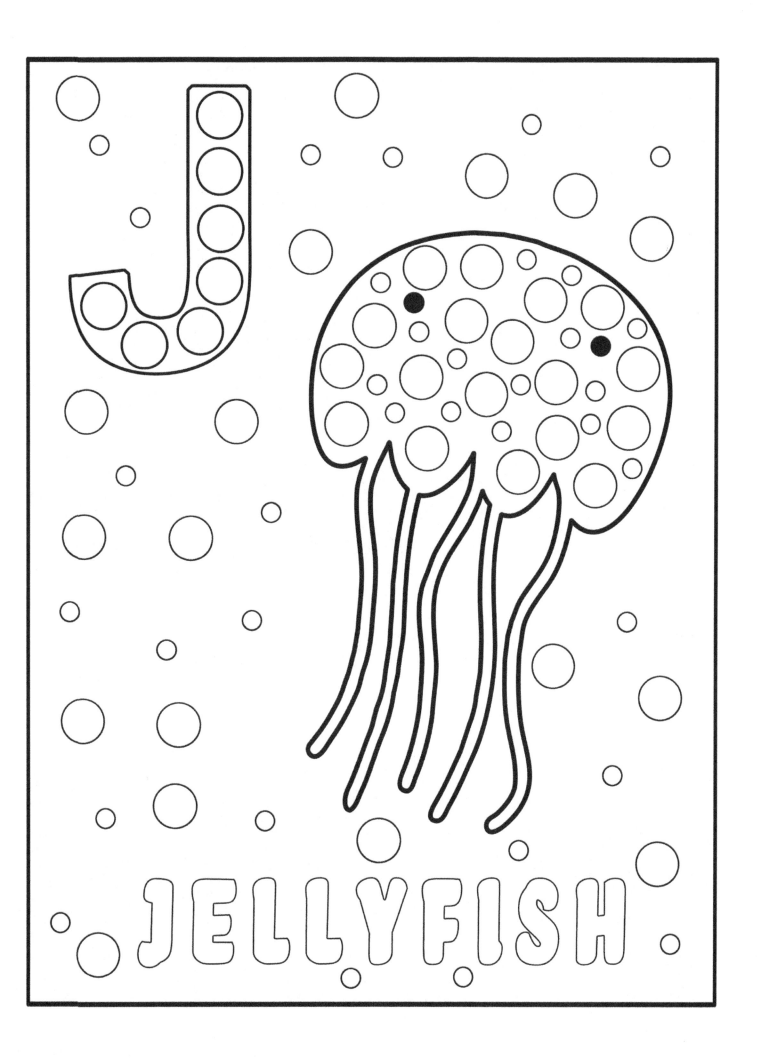

JELLYFISH

K

KILLER
WHALE

LOBSTER

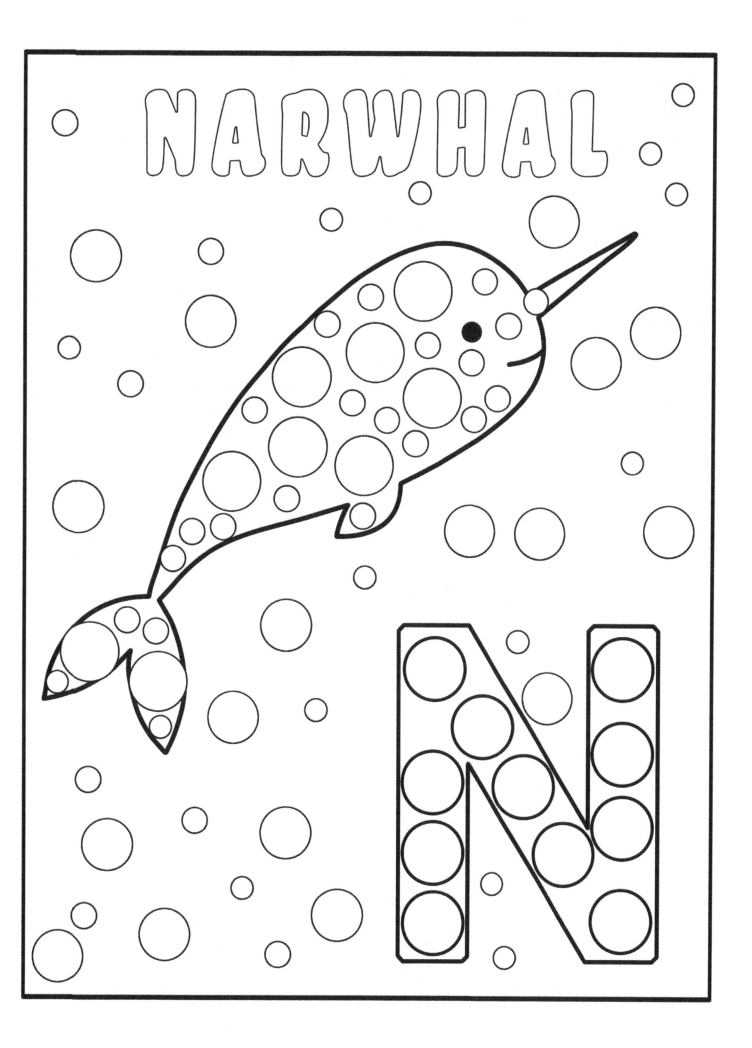

OCTOPUS

PENGUIN

QUILLFISH

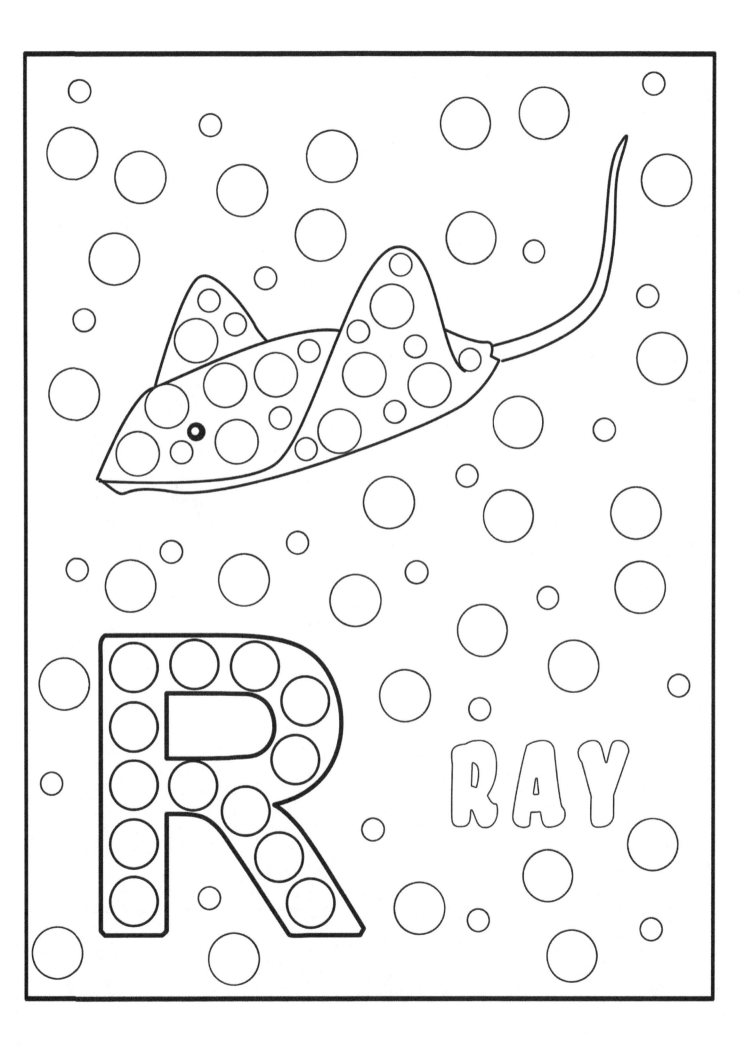

RAY

SEAHORSE

TURTLE

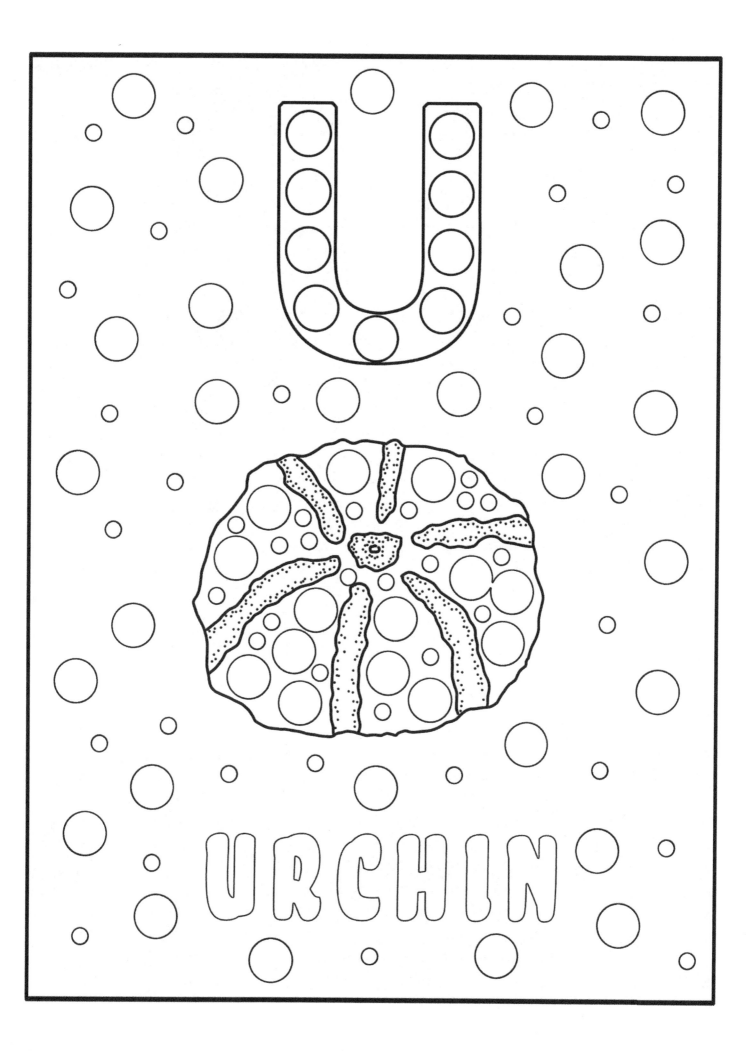

Y YELLOW TANG

THANK YOU SO MUCH!

Your Feedback is IMPORTANT to us!!!

We want to serve you better. We strive to
develop your kid's creativity and hand motor skills
so that they exercise their little brains
to their full potential with fun and happiness.

Kindly give us your suggestions to make our books better.
Please write to us at littlebrainpublishing@gmail.com

Don't Forget to give your honest REVIEW
of this book on AMAZON for
others to know about your experience.

How to Find the book?

TYPE **B08NYFXQ7T** on the Amazon Search Bar.
Pick this book and kindly rate us. Thanks ☺

little brain

About Us:

Shaping the future of our kids is in our hands.
Little Brain Publishing strives to exercise and develop
the little brain to its full potential.
Learning with fun and games is the best way to do so.

Kindly subscribe to our newsletter
for future book launches, printables,
freebies and blog articles.

Kindly make sure you open our mails
or visit our website frequently. Don't miss out.

Visit: www.littlebrainpublishing.com

Don't forget to claim your Christmas Coloring Bonus offer

Get yours here --> www.littlebrainpublishing.com/bonus

Made in the USA
Las Vegas, NV
28 November 2024

12833967R00037